POEMS FOR ME
THE MAD FAMILY

Families come in every shape and size — sometimes there are hundreds of uncles, aunts, cousins and second cousins, but sometimes there's just a mum (or dad) and child. Every family has its own interesting characters and its own special relationships — and all the fun and problems that go with them! In this entertaining and wide-ranging collection of poems for younger children, Tony Bradman takes a look at all the different sides of family life and at some of the people who make up the families, including some peculiar ones like Cousin Reggie, who surfboards down escalators, and the mother who lost her baby down the plughole! With contributions from Roger McGough, Allan Ahlberg, Tony Bradman himself and Spike Milligan, this is a strong contemporary anthology for all younger readers.

Tony Bradman is a freelance writer and journalist and a former deputy editor of *Parents* magazine. His first collection of original poetry, *Smile, Please!*, is also published in Puffin. He lives in London with his wife and three children.

Another book by Tony Bradman

SMILE, PLEASE!

POEMS FOR ME

THE MAD FAMILY

chosen by
TONY BRADMAN

Illustrated by
MADELEINE BAKER

PUFFIN BOOKS

PUFFIN BOOKS

Published by the Penguin Group
27 Wrights Lane, London W8 5TZ, England
Viking Penguin Inc., 40 West 23rd Street, New York, New York 10010, USA
Penguin Books Australia Ltd, Ringwood, Victoria, Australia
Penguin Books Canada Ltd, 2801 John Street, Markham, Ontario, Canada L3R 1B4
Penguin Books (NZ) Ltd, 182–190 Wairau Road, Auckland 10, New Zealand

Penguin Books Ltd, Registered Offices: Harmondsworth, Middlesex, England

First published by Blackie and Son Ltd 1987
Published in Puffin Books 1989
1 3 5 7 9 10 8 6 4 2

This collection copyright © Tony Bradman, 1987
Illustrations copyright © Madeleine Baker, 1987
All rights reserved

Made and printed in Great Britain by
Cox and Wyman Ltd, Reading, Berks
Filmset in Century Schoolbook Infant by
Rowland Phototypesetting Ltd, Bury St Edmunds, Suffolk

Except in the United States of America,
this book is sold subject to the condition
that it shall not, by way of trade or otherwise,
be lent, re-sold, hired out, or otherwise circulated
without the publisher's prior consent in any form of
binding or cover other than that in which it is
published and without a similar condition
including this condition being imposed
on the subsequent purchaser

In these pages you will find
Families of every kind.
Mums and dads, one in a pond,
Grans and grandpas of whom we're fond;
Uncles, aunts, a crazy cousin,
Brothers and sisters by the dozen;
Dozy brothers, arguing sisters,
Clever mothers, sisters with blisters,
Naughty children, whacky dads,
Uncles that would drive you mad;
Singing grannies, fathers alone,
Fights and fun inside the home.
All these things and more, you'll see,
Are what you'll find in families.
One more thing before you look –
Remember – we're *all* in this book!

Tony Bradman

The Mad Family

There was a mad man, he had a mad wife
And they lived in a mad town;
And they had children three at birth,
  And mad they were every one.
The father was mad, the mother was mad,
  And the children mad beside;
And they all got on a mad horse,
  And madly they did ride.
They rode by night and they rode by day,
  Yet never a one of them fell;
They rode so madly all the way
  Till they came to the gates of hell.
Old Nick was glad to see them so mad,
  And gladly let them in;
But he soon grew sorry to see them so
    merry
and let them out again.

Anon

Procession
(A skipping rhyme)

Here comes the bridegroom
Bride upon his arm,

Here comes the best man
Putting on the charm,
Winking at the bridesmaids
Dressed up very fine,
And trying to stop the little ones
From getting out of line;
Here come the mothers
In their fancy hats,
Walking with the fathers,
Having little chats,
Waving to the cousins
The uncles and the aunts,
The grandmas and the grandads
And a man in stripy pants;
Here come the work-mates,
Neighbours and the rest,
Friends of both families
All in their Sunday best;
Here comes the parson
Emptying the aisle,
Click, click, the cameras,
Everybody, everybody, everybody
    SMILE – cheese!

Anon

Thank You, Dad, for Everything

Thank you for laying the carpet, Dad,
Thank you for showing us how,
But what is that lump in the middle, Dad?
And why is it saying mia-ow?

Doug MacLeod

Appreciation

Auntie, did you feel no pain
Falling from that willow tree?
Will you do it, please, again?
'Cos my friend here didn't see.

Harry Graham

9

Uncle Jim

Oh, Matilda, look at your Uncle Jim,
He's in the bathtub learning how to
    swim
First he does the front stroke, then he
    does the side,
Now he's under water swimming against
    the tide.

Anon

Grandma Mabel

My Grandma Mabel's
Nice and jolly,
She gives me cakes
And sticky lollies.
Grandma Mabel
Baked a cake;
I ate the lot
And got tummy ache.
Grandma Mabel
Said to me
I'll boil the kettle
And make some tea.
Grandma Mabel's
Nice to me,
With cakes and smiles
And love for tea.

Tony Bradman

Grandpa John

When Grandpa John
Comes to tea,
He sits me on
His bony knees.
He tickles my chin
And tweaks my nose,
And tells me
I'm his little rose.
He tells me stories
And sings me songs,
He'll play with me
All day long.
And when it's time
To say goodbye,
Grandpa John says –
Hush, don't cry!

Tony Bradman

Granny Granny Please Comb My Hair

Granny Granny
please comb my hair
you always take your time
you always take such care

You put me to sit on a cushion
between your knees
you rub a little coconut oil
parting gentle as a breeze

Mummy Mummy
she's always in a hurry-hurry
rush
she pulls my hair
sometimes she tugs

But Granny
you have all the time in the world
and when you're finished
you always turn my head and say
'Now who's a nice girl.'

Grace Nichols

Be Nice to a New Baby

Be nice to a new baby,
I know it's not much fun:
She doesn't joke, won't play games,
And cannot even run.

She occupies your mother,
Who could be doing things
Like cutting out, or sticking down,
Or pushing you on swings.

Be kind to a new baby,
It might pay off in the end –
For that naggy little bundle
Could turn out to be a friend.

Fay Maschler

In Trouble

Whoever is caught
I get the blame
Wherever you go
I get into trouble.
If Tom and I was fighting
And get caught,
I will be the one to get into trouble,
And Tom gets a big cuddle.
It encourages him to do it again and
     again,
Even over the dinner table.
Whoever is naughty
I get the blame
And they get the cuddle.

Vivian Usherwood

Emma Hackett's Newsbook

Last night my mum
Got really mad
And threw a jam tart
At my dad.
Dad lost his temper
Then with mother,
Threw one at her
And hit my brother.
My brother thought
It was my sister,
Threw two at her
But somehow missed her.
My sister,
She is only three,
Hurled four at him
And one at me!
I said I wouldn't
Stand for that,
Aimed one at her
And hit the cat.
The cat jumped up
Like he'd been shot
And landed
In the baby's cot.

The baby —
Quietly sucking his thumb
Then started howling
For my mum.
At which my mum
Got really mad,
And threw a Swiss roll
At my dad.

Allan Ahlberg

High Heels

I wonder
how it feels
to wear high heels
like my big sister?

'Coz I'm smaller
I have to wait
longer
for high heels
to make me taller.

I wonder
how it feels
to wear high heels
and have corns
on your toes
and a blister?

I suppose
I'd better
ask my big sister.

John Agard

Our Mother

Our mother is a detective.
She is a great finder of clues.
She found the mud and grass on our
    shoes,
When we were told not to go in the park —
Because it would be getting dark —
But come straight home.
She found the jam on our thumbs,
And in our beds the tiniest crumbs
From the cakes we said we had not eaten.
When we blamed the cat for breaking the
    fruit bowl —
Because we did not want any fuss —
She *knew* it was us.

Allan Ahlberg

Daddy

Daddy lives in Tate Street now
he's got a flat
with patchy orange walls
and grey armchairs that
smell of someone else
And every Saturday we sleep there
Jo and me

Daddy lives in Tate Street now
he's got a flat
it's up a winding flight of stairs
it's cold and
dark at night it feels as though there's
no one there
not even Daddy Jo and me

Daddy lives in Tate Street now
he's got a flat
he grows tomatoes in a pot outside
and in a week or two
we'll help him put them on
a windowsill to ripen
Daddy says

Daddy lives in Tate Street now
he's got a flat
and we go out a lot
to films and fairs and
Christmas time he'll take us to
A Pantomime
he's promised

Daddy lives in Tate Street now
he's got a flat
he takes us home on Sunday
Mummy's in the kitchen Dick's there too
He's cooking something
Daddy says Goodbye
                    and then
goes home

Mick Gowar

You Were the Mother Last Time

'You were the mother last time.
It's my turn today.'
  'It's my turn.'
'No, *my* turn.'
  'All right then, I won't play.'
'Oh, go ahead then, *be* the mother.
It's not fair.
But I don't care.'

'I was the father last time.
I won't be today.'
  'It's your turn.'
'No, *your* turn.'

'All right then, I won't play.'
'Oh, never mind, *don't* be the father.
It's not fair.
But I don't care.'

'I was the sister last time.
It's your turn today.'
    'It is not.'
'It is so.'
    'All right then, I won't play.'
'Oh, never mind, *don't* be the sister.
It's not fair.
But I don't care.'

'I have an idea!
Let's both be mothers!
(We'll pretend
About the others.)'

Mary Ann Hoberman

Our Family

Sue works in a shop. John's driving a
   bus,
Joan's married to Frank and is not
   living with us,
Tom wants to leave school as soon as he
   can,
Father still speaks like a west
   countryman;
So that's all of us, with Mother and me,
In our family.

Crystella's from Cyprus, George, Port of
   Spain,
His father talks cricket and works on a
   crane,
Lynn, born in Jamaica, is slender and
   tall,
Fazi wears earrings and comes from
   Bengal;
So that's some of them, their mothers,
   and me,
In our family.

Leonard Clark

Music Makers

My auntie plays the piccolo,
My uncle plays the flute,
They practise every night at ten,
Tweetly tweet *Toot-toot*!

My granny plays the banjo,
My grandad plays the drum,
They practise every night at nine,
Plankety plank *Bumm-bumm*!!

My sister plays the tuba,
My brother plays guitar,
They practise every night at six,
Twankity *Oom-pa-pa*!!!

My mother plays the mouth organ,
My daddy plays oboe,
They practise every night at eight,
Pompity-pom suck-blow!!!!

Spike Milligan

Going Through the Old Photos

Who's that?
That's your Auntie Mabel
and that's me
under the table.

Who's that?
That's Uncle Billy.
Who's that?
Me being silly.

Who's that
licking a lolly?
I'm not sure
but I think it's Polly.

Who's that
behind the tree?
I don't know,
I can't see.
Could be you.
Could be me.

Who's that?
Baby Joe.
Who's that?
I don't know.

Who's that standing
on his head?
Turn it round.
It's Uncle Ted.

Mike Rosen

Cousin Reggie

Cousin Reggie
who adores the sea
lives in the Midlands
unfortunately.

He surfs down escalators
in department stores
and swims the High Street
on all of his fours.

Sunbathes on the pavement
paddles in the gutter
(I think our Reggie's
a bit of a nutter).

Roger McGough

Speak Roughly to Your Little Boy

'Speak roughly to your little boy,
    And beat him when he sneezes;
He only does it to annoy,
    Because he knows it teases.'

Chorus:
    'Wow! Wow! Wow!'

'I speak severely to my boy,
    I beat him when he sneezes;
For he can thoroughly enjoy
    The pepper when he pleases!'

Chorus:
    'Wow! Wow! Wow!'

Lewis Carroll

Four Children

William and Mary,
   George and Anne,
Four such children
   Had never a man;
They put their father
   To flight and shame
And called their brother
   A shocking bad name.

Anon

Just Fancy That

'Just fancy that!' my parents say
At anything I mention.
They always seem so far away
And never pay attention.

30

'Just fancy that,' their eyes are glazed.
It grows so very wearing.
'Just fancy that' is not a line
For which I'm really caring.

And so today I'm telling them
I threw a cricket bat.
I broke a windowpane at school.
They murmur, 'Fancy that.'

I wrote a message on the fence.
I spoke a wicked word.
The way the vicar hurried past,
I'm positive he heard.

'Just fancy that.' Then suddenly
Their eyes are sticking out,
Their words are coming in a rush,
Their voices in a shout.

'You naughty child, you shameless boy,
It's time WE had a chat.'
Hurrah, they've noticed me at last.
My goodness, fancy that!

Max Fatchen

My Sister Laura

My sister Laura's bigger than me
And lifts me up quite easily.
I can't lift her, I've tried and tried:
She must have something heavy inside.

Spike Milligan

Celia

Celia always took her time
Over what she had to do.
She'd take at least six minutes
Just to fasten up one shoe.

To find her coat would be a task
Of many minutes more;
It could be half an hour
Before Celia reached the door.

'Please *hurry*' and 'Don't *dawdle*'
Meant nothing to that child.
Celia always took her time
To drive her parents wild.

Fay Maschler

An Argument

Molly, my sister, and I fell out
And what do you think it was all about?
She loved coffee and I loved tea,
And that was the reason we couldn't
   agree.

Anon

My Brother Tommy

When my brother Tommy
Sleeps in bed with me
He doubles up
And makes
himself
exactly
like
a
V
And 'cause the bed is not so wide
A part of him is on my side.

A. B. Ross

Billy Is Blowing His Trumpet

Billy is blowing his trumpet;
Bertie is banging a tin;
Betty is crying for Mummy
And Bob has pricked Ben with a pin.
Baby is crying out loudly;
He's out on the lawn in his pram.
I am the only one silent
And I've eaten all of the jam.

Anon

Jack and Jill

Jack and Jill
Went up the hill
To fetch a pail of water;
Jack fell down,
And broke his crown,
And Jill came tumbling after.

Up Jack got,
And home did trot,
As fast as he could caper;
To old Dame Dob,
Who patched his nob
With vinegar and brown paper.

When Jill came in,
How she did grin
To see Jack's paper plaster;
Her mother, vexed,
Did whip her next,
For laughing at Jack's disaster.

Now Jack did laugh
And Jill did cry,
But her tears did soon abate;
Then Jill did say,
That she should play
At see-saw across the gate.

Anon

The Angels' Lament

A mother was bathing her baby one
   night,
The youngest of ten and a tiny young
   mite.
The mother was poor and the baby was
   thin,
'Twas naught but a skelington covered
   in skin.
The mother turned round for the soap off
   the rack,
She was but a moment, but when she
   turned back,
The baby was gone – and in anguish she
   cried,
'Oh, where is my baby?' . . . the angels
   replied . . .

'Your baby has gone down the plug hole,
Your baby has gone down the plug;
The poor little thing was so skinny and
   thin,
He should have been bathed in a jug . . .
           In a jug!

'Your baby is perfectly happy,
He won't need a bath any more;
Your baby has gone down the plug hole,
Not lost – but gone before . . .
He's gone before!'

Anon

Newcomers

My father came to England
from another country
My father's mother came to England
from another country
but my father's father
stayed behind.

So my dad had no dad here
and I never saw him at all.

One day in spring
some things arrived:
a few old papers,
a few old photos
and – oh yes –
a hulky bulky thick checked jacket
that belonged to the man
I would have called 'Grandad'.
The Man Who Stayed Behind.

But I kept that jacket
and I wore it
and I wore it
and I wore it
till it wore right through
at the back.

Mike Rosen

Extremely Naughty Children

By far
The naughtiest
Children
I know
Are Jasper
Geranium
James
and Jo.

They live
In a house
On the hill
Of Kidd,
And what
In the world
Do you think
They did?

They asked
Their uncles
And aunts
To tea,
And shouted
In loud
Rude voices
'We

Are tired
Of scoldings
And sendings
To bed:
Now
The grown-ups
Shall be
Punished instead.'

They said:
'Auntie Em,
You didn't
Say "Thank you!"'
They said:
'Uncle Robert,
We're going
To spank you!'

They pulled
The beard
Of Sir Henry
Dorner
And put him
To stand
In disgrace
In the corner.

They scolded
Aunt B,
They punished
Aunt Jane;
They slapped
Aunt Louisa
Again
And again.

They said
'Naughty boy!'
To their
Uncle Fred,
And boxed
His ears
And sent him
To bed.

Do you think
Aunts Em
And Loo
And B,
And Sir
Henry
Dorner
(KCB),

And the elderly
Uncles
And kind
Aunt Jane
Will go
To tea
With the children
Again?

Elizabeth Godley

The Older the Violin the Sweeter the Tune

Me Granny old
Me Granny wise
Stories shine like the moon
from inside she eyes.

Me Granny can dance
Me Granny can sing
but she can't play violin.

Yet she always saying
'Dih older dih violin
de sweeter de tune.'

Me Granny must be wiser
than the man inside the moon.

John Agard

Dads

I tell you, sometimes I get really mad
When other kids talk about their dads.
I haven't got a dad, you see;
There's just my mum and me.

Most of the time I really don't mind,
And I'm sure they don't mean to be
   unkind.
I haven't got a dad, you see;
But it's all right, just mum and me.
Though sometimes they just rabbit on,
About the things their dads have done.
And I haven't got a dad, you see,
To do those things for mum and me.

But I won't care, I really won't,
If they talk about dads or if they don't.
I haven't got a dad, you see.
There's just my mum – just my mum and
   me.

Tony Bradman

I Had a Little Brother

I had a little brother
His name was Tiny Tim;
I put him in the bathtub
To teach him how to swim.
He drank up all the water,
He ate up all the soap,
He died last night
With a bubble in his throat.
In came the doctor,
In came the nurse,
In came the lady
With the alligator purse.

Dead said the doctor,
Dead said the nurse,
Dead said the lady
With the alligator purse.
Out went the doctor,
Out went the nurse,
Out went the lady
With the alligator purse.

But then my little brother
Whose name was Tiny Tim
Sat up upon his little bed

And gave us all a grin.
He ate up all his dinner,
He drank up all his drink,
He laughed and laughed
Until he cried, and then –

What do you think?
In came the doctor,
In came the nurse,
In came the lady
With the alligator purse.
Good said the doctor,
Good said the nurse,
Good said the lady
With the alligator purse.

Then out went the doctor,
Out went the nurse,
And out went the lady
With the alligator purse!

Anon and Tony Bradman

Little Girl

Little girl, little girl,
    Where have you been?
I've been to see grandmother
    Over the green.
What did she give you?
    Milk in a can.
What did you say for it?
    Thank you, Grandam.

Anon

Grandad

Grandad's dead
And I'm sorry about that

He'd a huge black overcoat.
He felt proud in it.
You could have hidden
A football crowd in it.
Far too big —
It was a lousy fit
But Grandad didn't
Mind a bit.

He wore it all winter
With a squashed black hat.

*Now he's dead
And I'm sorry about that.*

He'd got twelve stories.
I'd heard every one of them
Hundreds of times
But that was the fun of them:
You knew what was coming
So you could join in.
He'd got big hands
And brown, grooved skin
And when he laughed
It knocked you flat.

*Now he's dead
And I'm sorry about that.*

Kit Wright

I'm Alone in the Evening

I'm alone in the evening
when the family sits
reading and sleeping
and I watch the fire in close
to see flame goblins
wriggling out of their caves
for the evening

Later I'm alone
when the bath has gone cold around me
and I have put my foot
beneath the cold tap
where it can dribble
through valleys between my toes
out across the white plain of my foot
and bibble bibble into the sea

I'm alone
when mum's switched out the light
my head against the pillow
listening to ca thump ca thump
in the middle of my ears.
It's my heart.

Mike Rosen

Daddy Fell into the Pond

Everyone grumbled. The sky was grey.
We had nothing to do and nothing to say.
We were nearing the end of a dismal day.
And there seemed to be nothing beyond.
    Then
        Daddy fell into the pond!

And everyone's face grew merry and
    bright,
And Timothy danced for sheer delight.
'Give me the camera, quick, oh quick!
He's crawling out of the duckweed!' Click!

Then the gardener suddenly slapped his
    knee,
And doubled up, shaking silently,
And the ducks all quacked as if they were
    daft,
And it sounded as if the old drake
    laughed.

Oh, there wasn't a thing that didn't respond
When
Daddy fell into the pond!

Alfred Noyes

The Old Woman in a Shoe

There was an old woman who lived in a
   shoe,
She had so many children, she didn't
   know what to do;
She gave them some broth without any
   bread,
She whipped them all soundly and put
   them to bed.

Anon

Index of First Lines

Acknowledgements

The publishers and author would like to thank the following for their kind permission to reproduce copyright material in this book:

The Bodley Head for 'The Older the Violin the Sweeter the Tune' and 'High Heels' by John Agard from *Say It Again, Granny* and *I Din Do Nuttin*; Penguin Books for 'Our Mother' and 'Emma Hackett's Newsbook' by Allan Ahlberg from *Please Mrs Butler* (Kestrel Books, 1983), copyright © 1983 by Allan Ahlberg; The Estate of Leonard Clark for 'Our Family' by Leonard Clark; The Estate of A. B. Ross for 'My Brother Tommy' by A. B. Ross; Penguin Books for 'Just Fancy That' by Max Fatchen from *Wry Rhymes for Trouble-some Times* (Kestrel Books, 1983), copyright © 1983 by Max Fatchen; The Bodley Head for 'Extremely Naughty Children' by Elizabeth Godley from *Green Outside*; William Collins and Sons Ltd for 'Daddy' by Mick Gowar from *Swings and Roundabouts*; Russell & Volkening Inc. as agents for the author for 'You Were the Mother Last Time' by Mary Ann Hoberman © 1965 by Mary Ann Hoberman; Penguin Books Australia and Doug MacLeod for 'Thank You Dad for Everything' by Doug MacLeod from *The Fed Up Family Album*; Methuen London for 'Cousin Reggie' by Roger McGough from *Sporting Relations*; Jonathan Cape for 'Be Nice to a New Baby' and 'Celia' by Fay Maschler from *A Child's Book of Manners*, text copyright © Fay Maschler, 1978; Spike Milligan for 'Music Makers' from *Unspun Socks from a Chicken's Laundry*, published by Michael Joseph; Penguin Books for 'My Sister Laura' by Spike Milligan from *Silly Verse for Kids*; the author for 'Granny Granny Please Comb My Hair' by Grace Nichols from *I Like That Stuff* selected by Morag Styles, published by OUP; Blackwood Pillans and Wilson for 'Daddy Fell into the Pond' by Alfred Noyes; Penguin Books for 'Going Through the Old Photos' by Michael Rosen, from *You Tell Me*, poems by Roger McGough and Michael Rosen (Kestrel Books, 1979), Michael Rosen poems copyright © 1979 by Michael Rosen, collection copyright © 1979 by Penguin Books; André Deutsch for

'Newcomers' by Michael Rosen from *Quick Let's Get Out of Here*; Centerprise Publications for 'In Trouble' by Vivian Usherwood; William Collins and Sons for 'Grandad' by Kit Wright from *Rabbiting On*. Every effort has been made to trace copyright holders and the publishers and author apologize if any inadvertent omission has been made.

ONE NIL
Tony Bradman

Dave Brown is mad about football and when he learns that the England squad are to train at the local City ground he thinks up a brilliant plan to overcome his parents' objections and get him to the ground to see them.

ON THE NIGHT WATCH
Hannah Cole

A group of children and their parents occupy their tiny school in an effort to prevent its closure.

FIONA FINDS HER TONGUE
Diana Hendry

At home Fiona is a chatterbox, but whenever she goes out she just won't say a word. How she overcomes her shyness and 'finds her tongue' is told in this charming book.

IT'S TOO FRIGHTENING FOR ME!
Shirley Hughes

The eerie old house gives Jim and Arthur the creeps. But somehow they just can't resist poking around it, even when a mysterious white face appears at the window! A deliciously scary story – for brave readers only!

THE CONKER AS HARD AS A DIAMOND
Chris Powling

Last conker season Little Alpesh had lost every single game! But this year it's going to be different and he's going to be Conker Champion of the Universe! The trouble is, only a conker as hard as a diamond will make it possible – and where on earth is he going to find one?

THE GHOST AT NO. 13

Gyles Brandreth

Hamlet Brown's sister, Susan, is just too perfect. Everything she does is praised and Hamlet is in despair – until a ghost comes to stay for a holiday and helps him to find an exciting idea for his school project!

RADIO DETECTIVE

John Escott

A piece of amazing deduction by the Roundbay Radio Detective when Donald, the radio's young presenter, solves a mystery but finds out more than anyone expects.

RAGDOLLY ANNA'S CIRCUS

Jean Kenward

Made only from a morsel of this and a tatter of that, Ragdolly Anna is a very special doll and the six stories in this book are all about her adventures.

SEE YOU AT THE MATCH

Margaret Joy

Six delightful stories about football. Whether spectator, player, winner or loser these short, easy stories for young readers are a must for all football fans.

PUFFIN COVER COVER STORY TAPES

Some complete and unabridged Puffin/ cover to cover tapes currently available: